Eb BARITONE SAXOPHONE

CONCERT FAVORITES

Volume 1

Band Arrangements Correlated with
Essential Elements Band Method Book 1

ISBN 978-0-634-05207-1

HAL•LEONARD®
7777 W. BLUEMOUND RD. P.O. BOX 13819 MILWAUKEE, WI 53213

00860127

LET'S ROCK!

Eb BARITONE SAXOPHONE

MICHAEL SWEENEY (ASCA

Shout:

Let's Rock!

MAJESTIC MARCH

BARITONE SAXOPHONE

By PAUL LAVENDER

March Tempo

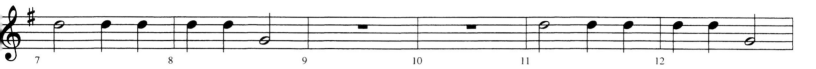

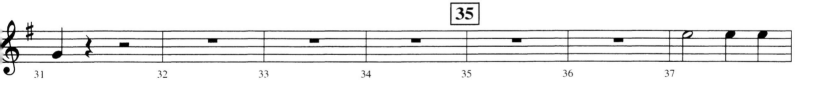

860127

MICKEY MOUSE MARCH
(From Walt Disney's "THE MICKEY MOUSE CLUB")

E♭ BARITONE SAXOPHONE

Words and Music by JIMMIE DODD
Arranged by MICHAEL SWEENEY

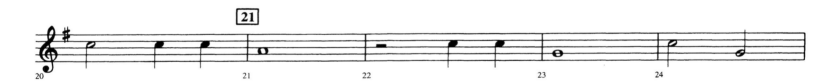

POWER ROCK

(We Will Rock You • Another One Bites The Dust)

Eb BARITONE SAXOPHONE

Arranged by MICHAEL SWEENEY

860127

WHEN THE SAINTS GO MARCHING IN

Words by KATHERINE E. PUR
Music by JAMES M. BLA
Arranged by JOHN HIGGIN

E♭ BARITONE SAXOPHONE

FARANDOLE
(From "L'Arlésienne")

Eb BARITONE SAXOPHONE

GEORGES BIZET
Arranged by MICHAEL SWEENEY (ASCAP)

860127

JUS' PLAIN BLUES

E♭ BARITONE SAXOPHONE

MICHAEL SWEENEY (ASCAP)

From the Paramount and Twentieth Century Fox Motion Picture TITANIC

MY HEART WILL GO ON

(Love Theme From 'Titanic')

Music by JAMES HORNER
Lyric by WILL JENNINGS
Arranged by PAUL LAVENDER

E♭ BARITONE SAXOPHONE

00860127

From THE MUPPET MOVIE

THE RAINBOW CONNECTION

Words and Music by PAUL WILLIAMS
and KENNITH L. ASCHER
Arranged by PAUL LAVENDER

E♭ BARITONE SAXOPHONE

00860127

From Walt Disney's MARY POPPINS

SUPERCALIFRAGILISTICEXPIALIDOCIOUS

Words and Music by
RICHARD M. SHERMAN and ROBERT B. SHERMAN
Arranged by MICHAEL SWEENEY

E♭ **BARITONE SAXOPHONE**

00860127

(From "THE SOUND OF MUSIC")
DO-RE-MI

Eb BARITONE SAXOPHONE

Lyrics by OSCAR HAMMERSTEIN II
Music by RICHARD RODGERS
Arranged by PAUL LAVENDER

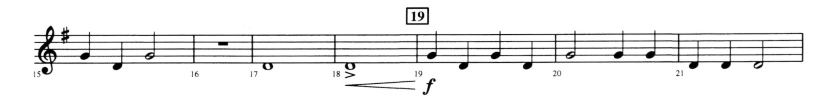

DRUMS OF CORONA

E♭ BARITONE SAXOPHONE

MICHAEL SWEENEY (ASCAP)

00860127

LAREDO
(Concert March)

Eb BARITONE SAXOPHONE

JOHN HIGGINS

POMP AND CIRCUMSTANCE
March No. 1

Eb BARITONE SAXOPHONE

By EDWARD ELGAR
Arranged by MICHAEL SWEENEY

0860127

STRATFORD MARCH

E♭ BARITONE SAXOPHONE

JOHN HIGGINS (ASCAP)